1 Space Camp Florida

W0357446

1 ▶ American crosswords

a *Complete the crossword.*

1 American money
2 The British write 'programme'.
3 The British say 'form' or 'class'.
4 When you go to a new country and visit lots of places there, you …
5 Americans who speak Spanish at home.
6 A party where you cook and eat outside.
7 You'll find one outside lots of US buildings.

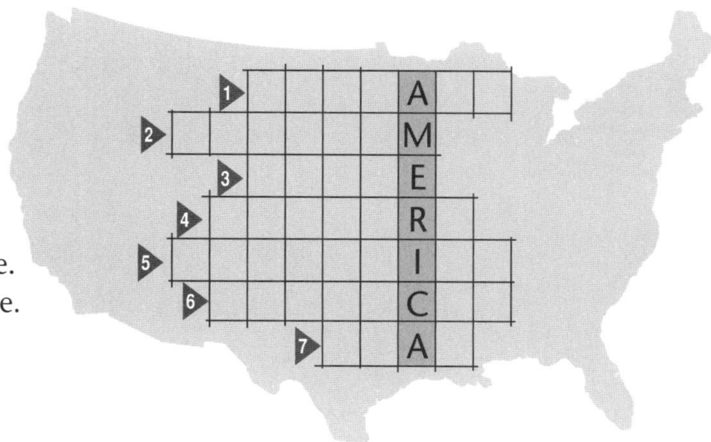

b *This time write the clues.*

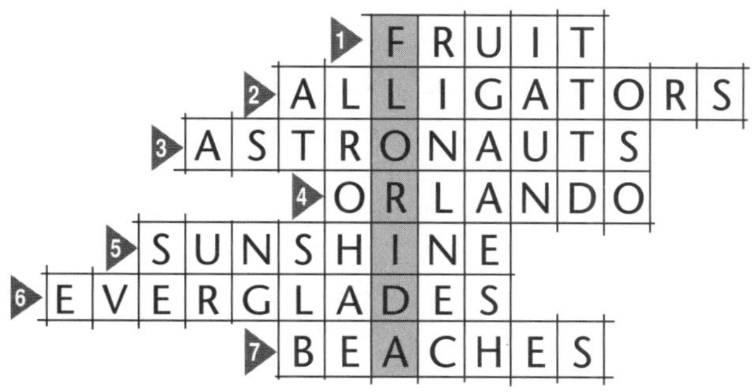

1 ______________________

____

2 ______________________

____

3 ______________________

____

4 ______________________

5 ______________________

6 ______________________

7 ______________________

▶▶▶ NOW YOU

Make your own crossword. Think of some words and write the clues. Perhaps a partner could complete your crossword?

1 ________ U ________
2 ________ S ________
3 ________ A ________

1 ______________________

____

____

2 ______________________

____

____

3 ______________________

____

____

p. 9

2 BLUE BOX British and American English → blue box, p. 141

These sentences were written by an American. The spelling of one word in each sentence is different in British English (BE). Underline that word. Then write it again with BE spelling.

tip If you need help with the 'blue box' exercises, look at the vocabulary at the back of your pupil's book.

1 I never go to the <u>theater</u>. *theatre* ____________
2 Who is your favorite singer? ____________
3 Pink is a nice color. ____________
4 Do you say 'miles' or 'kilometers'? ____________
5 How far is it to the center of the city? ____________
6 I traveled by plane. ____________
7 I'd love to see New York harbor. ____________

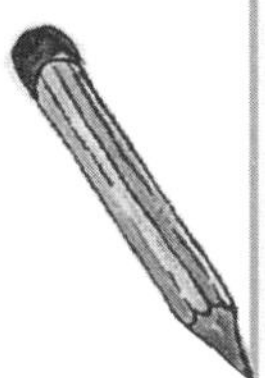

3 ▶ Telephone language

Sabine Müller is trying to ring her brother, Jan.
He is staying with an English family. Complete the dialogues.

MAN Hello?
SABINE Oh, erm ... ____________ 792356?
MAN No, it isn't.
SABINE Oh, sorry. ____________________________

ANSWER-PHONE This is 792356. We can't answer the phone at the moment. ____________________ after the beep. Thanks.
SABINE Oh nein, es ist der Anrufbeantworter!

WOMAN Hello?
SABINE Hello. ____________________________
I'm Jan's sister. ____________________ to Jan, please?
WOMAN I'm sorry, Jan's out. ____________________ a message?
SABINE It's OK, thanks. ____________________________

Later ...

WOMAN Hello?
SABINE Hello. Is Jan there, please?
WOMAN ____________________________
SABINE Oh sorry. It's Sabine, Jan's sister.
WOMAN Oh, of course. ____________________________
I'll get him.

p. 10/A1, p.15/P6

4 ▶ A postcard to a friend

Read the postcard on the right. Then imagine you are on holiday. Choose one of the other postcards and write it to a friend.
Write

... where you are,
... what you're doing there,
... what the weather's like,
... what you're doing the next day.

Dear Jane,
Hi from the USA! I'm having a super time. This place is great. The course is a bit hard. But it's fun — much better than school. The weather is fine every day. I'm leaving tomorrow. My parents and I are going on a trip round Florida before we come home. Say hi to your mum.
Love Margo
PS: Don't forget to send me a postcard.

To
Jane Harr
43, Sulliv
London St
England

p. 11/A2

5 ▶ How strict are your parents?

Write about the things your parents let you do – and don't let you do. What do they make you do? What don't they make you do? The ideas in the box can help you.

- do jobs at home
- stay out as late as you want
- have parties when they're out
- pay for your own sports equipment
- write thank you letters to relatives
- choose the clothes you like
- bring a friend on holiday
- go on holiday on your own
- ...

p. 11/A2

6 ▶ Pick it up!

Look at the pictures. What are the people saying?
Write a sentence for each picture.
Use the verbs in the box.

cut out • pick up • put down
put on • throw away • turn off
wake up • write down

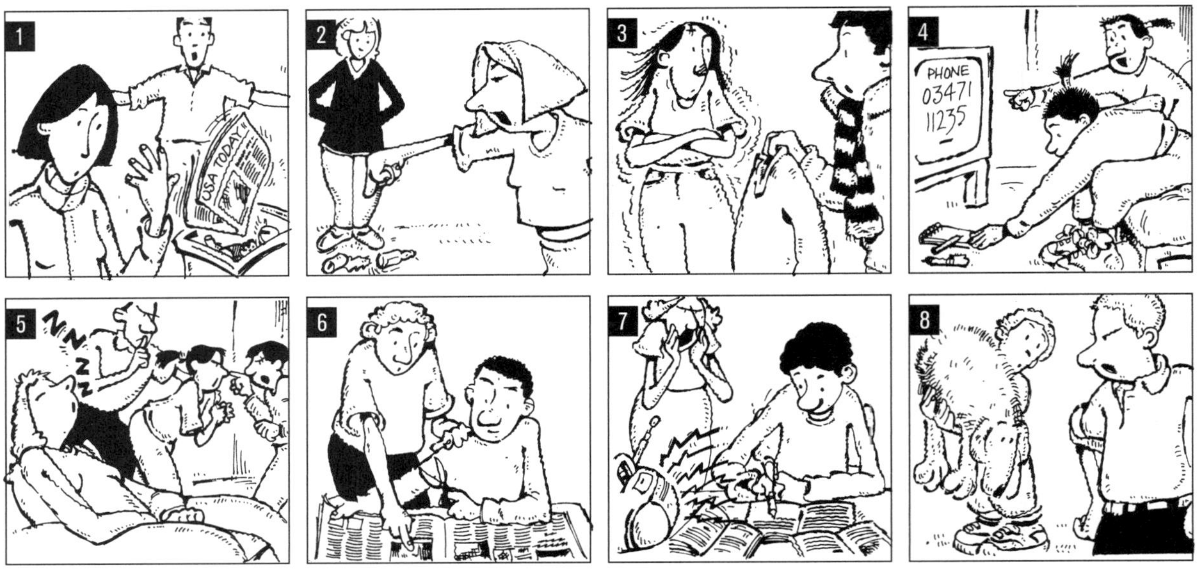

1 *Don't throw it away!*
2 ______
3 ______
4 ______
5 ______
6 ______
7 ______
8 ______

p. 12/A5

7 ▶ A space tragedy

Complete the text with the verbs in the box.

appear • arrive • beat • become
climb • count • happen • look
push • speak • stand

It was a cold morning in January 1986. At the Kennedy Space Center, a group of people stood together and watched the sun *appear* at last. I sat at my desk in the Center as usual. We were all waiting for something important. On my screen I saw seven people ______ in a large hall. They were ready for their mission. I noticed the seven ______ in front of the rocket and ______ at it one last time. I heard nobody ______ in the Space Center for a minute or two. Then the seven people were in the rocket and we all listened to the famous voice ______ the numbers: '10, 9, 8, 7, ...'. I felt the whole Center ______ tense in those last seconds. Then we all watched that beautiful rocket ______ up into the air. We heard the noisy engines ______ the huge thing higher and higher. And for 73 seconds we felt our hearts ______ faster and faster – before we watched a terrible tragedy ______ in front of our eyes.

p. 12/A5

8 SOUNDS Stressed syllables

Say these words. Where's the stress? Put them into the correct list.

American • astronaut • attraction
community • except • exciting
explore • Hispanic • important • interested
menu • nervous • planet
prefer • programme • project • religion
restaurant • serious • student

stress on the first syllable as in 'holiday'		stress on the second syllable as in 'vacation'	
astronaut	______	*American*	______
______	______	______	______
______	______	______	______
______	______	______	______
______	______	______	______

p. 12/A5

9 ▶ At the fast food kiosk

Complete the conversation. (Tip: Look at the green box on page 122 of your pupil's book for help.)

MAN AT KIOSK Was hat er? Ich habe keine Ahnung. Kannst du ihn verstehen?

YOU Can I help?

TOURIST Oh dear, I can't understand this menu.

YOU Er sagt, ______________________________ .

MAN Frag ihn, was er essen will.

YOU ______________________________

TOURIST I'd like something German. I can eat a hamburger at home.

YOU ______________________________

MAN Wie wäre es mit einer Currywurst?

YOU ______________________________

TOURIST What's a 'Currywurst'?

YOU ______________________________

TOURIST Fine. I'll have one of those and I'd like some chips, too, please. No salt.

YOU ______________________________

MAN Alles klar. Das macht € 2,50.

YOU ______________________________

TOURIST Great. Thanks very much for your help.

p. 12/A5

WORKING WITH THE TEXT

10 ▶ What happens in the story?

Finish these sentences and summarize the story on pages 16/17.

After the trip to Space Camp, Conchita wants to ______________________________

____.

When Conchita goes back to school, ______________________________

____.

Her teacher says the other kids are jealous because ______________________________

____.

When Conchita gives her talk about Space Camp, ______________________________

____.

But most people in the class ______________________________

____.

At the end of the story, ______________________________

____.

11 ▶ Everybody's talking

a *After the Science class, everybody is talking about Conchita. Who might say these things?*

1 Hey Linda, Conchita thinks she's so special. She thinks, 'I'm so great, and you guys are so ordinary.' You called her little Miss Astronaut too. And her talk was so boring. Why are you friends with her again? José is angry with you!

2 I think it's really great that Conchita won that scholarship to Space Camp. It was hard for her because some of the other kids in the class were horrible to her. She was sad at first, but I think she has learned something very important.

Person 1 might be ____________________. Person 2 might be ____________________.

b *Imagine you are Mike. What would you say?*

____

____

____

____

____

____

____

p. 16/17

Unit 1 NOW YOU CAN ...

12 ▶ ... talk with kids at school in English

How do you say these things in English?

1 Was hast du denn?

____

2 Halte durch!

____

3 Halt den Mund und hör zu!

____

4 Geht meine Uhr richtig? Ist es erst 11 Uhr?

____

5 Dein Buch ist verkehrt herum.

____

13 ▶ ... do this crossword

1 a The American word for 'autumn' — _ _ L L
b A very big room — _ _ L L

2 a You go here to get a plane. — _ I R _ _ _ _
b When you really want something — _ _ _ I R _

3 a 'My train arrives at 6 pm.'
– 'OK. I'll come and ... you.' — M E _ _
b The list of things you can eat in a restaurant — M E _ _

4 a You do this when you are tired. — _ A W _
b An AE word for 'great' or 'fantastic' — A W _ _ _ _ _

14 ▶ ... write about someone you met

Think of an interesting person that you met somewhere. Perhaps you were on holiday, on a school trip, at a party, etc. The questions in the box can help you.

- Where did you meet this person?
- What did you like about him/her?
- What did you do together?
- Did you see him/her again after that?
- Did you write/ phone?
- Why/Why not?

____

Unit 1 How to present an argument

1 ▶ For or against?

List the phrases you can use to give an opinion under the headings in the table.

All in all • Don't forget • I don't agree with • I hate
I have a problem with • I wish there were more • I'm a big fan
I'm against • I'm for • If you ask me • In my experience
In my opinion • It's ... that I don't like • Just remember
What I don't like is

Saying you are **for** something (3)	Saying you are **against** something (6)	General 'argument' phrases (6)
______	______	______
______	______	______
______	______	______
	______	______
	______	______
	______	______

2 ▶ Young people's opinions on summer camps

Complete these sentences with phrases from the box. Sometimes more than one phrase is possible.

1 ______ going away to summer camps. They're always the same.

2 ______, the food at summer camps is awful.

3 ______, summer camps are great for people who like meeting other people.

4 ______ summer camps. Parents just want to get rid of their kids.

5 ______ summer camps. I can't stand the rules.

6 ______: it's always nice to do things with people.

7 ______: the weather is so important.

8 ______, the summer holidays are boring. So summer camp is something to look forward to.

9 ______ getting up early ______.

10 ______ that there's always somebody horrible there. And you have to live with them for weeks.

11 You make good friends. ______ summer camps.

12 I look forward to summer camp every year – it's lots of fun. ______ of them.

13 ______ summer camps. They're too expensive and not everyone can go.

14 ______ summer camps in this country.

15 ______, there's something for everybody.

3 ▶ Your opinion

What do you think of summer camps? Have you ever been to one? Are there any in your area? Would you like to go to one? What would you like about them? What would you not like? In your exercise book, write a paragraph about what you think. You can be for or against – or both.

2 Alaska – the Great Land

1 ▶ **Did you hear it happen?**
Look at the picture on pages 20/21 of your pupil's book. What did you 'hear', 'see' and 'feel' on the imaginary journey to Alaska? Write sentences.
I could (not) hear / see / feel …

grasses • plane
school • tools • truck
wind • woman • …

blow on my face
break under my feet
click • disappear • sing
start • take off •
work • …

____

____

____

____

____

____ p. 21

2 **REVISION** Glen's Space Camp diary
Complete the paragraph with verbs from the box. Use the simple past.

be × 3 • build • go • have • look
(not) be • (not) fly • (not) get up
(not) like • wake up • watch • write

MONDAY

I __________ at 7 o'clock, but I ________________ until 7.30. I _____ breakfast in the 'Milky Way Café' with the other kids in my team. The food _____ OK, but I ____________ the bread. Josh and I ______ a bit late for training. The counsellor ________ pleased! In the afternoon we ______ a great rocket. Well, it _________ great, but it ____________ very well! The others ___________ a film in the evening, but I ______ to bed early and _______ a letter to my family. It _____ a good day.

▶▶▶ **NOW YOU**
Write your diary for one day last week.

____

____

____

____

____

____

2

3 REVISION Glen's photo album

a *Glen is showing a friend some photos. What is he saying? Use the* present perfect *and* since *or* for.

1 We – live – Anchorage – 1997

We have lived in ______________________________ .

2 – father – work here – engineer – then.

My father ______________________________

______________________________ .

3 Here's a picture of my mom. (– parents – be – divorced – more than five years)

My parents ______________________________ .

4 That's my sister Amy with her friend Judy. (– know – each other – they were kids)

They ______________________________ .

5 That's a girl I met at Space Camp. (– write – me two letters – I got back)

She ______________________________ .

b *Now he's calling his mum on the phone. What is he saying? Use the* present perfect progressive.

1 Amy is cross with me. She and I (fight) *have been fighting*.

2 It's 8 o'clock and Dad still isn't home. He (work) ______________ since 8 o'clock this morning.

3 I'm feeling tired. I (learn) ______________ for a test.

4 Amy is stupid. She (try) ______________ to learn Inupiaq for weeks.

4 ▶ Before Space Camp

Match the sentence halves. Then put the verbs in brackets in the simple past *or the* past perfect.

1 After Glen (see) ______________ a TV programme about Space Camp,

2 Glen (not, talk) ______________ to his dad about going to Space Camp

3 Glen (be) ______________ really interested

4 After Glen (read) ______________ about Space Camp scholarships,

5 When Glen (write) ______________ his letter,

6 Glen (be) ______________ a bit nervous before his trip to Florida

- until he (find) ______________ some more information on the internet.
- because he (always, want) ______________ ______________ to travel.
- he (ask) ______________ his teacher for more information .
- because he (never, travel) ______________ ______________ alone before.
- he (decide) ______________ to write a letter and ask for one.
- he (wait) ______________ nervously for the answer.

p. 22/A2

5 BLUE BOX The German word 'man' → blue box, p. 146

Which words can you translate with 'man'? (Circle) them.

6 ▶ A talk on whaling

Imagine your Science teacher has asked you and a partner to give a talk on whaling. You have found some information on the Internet – but it's in English. Complete the conversation. (Tip: Look at page 122 of your pupil's book for help.)

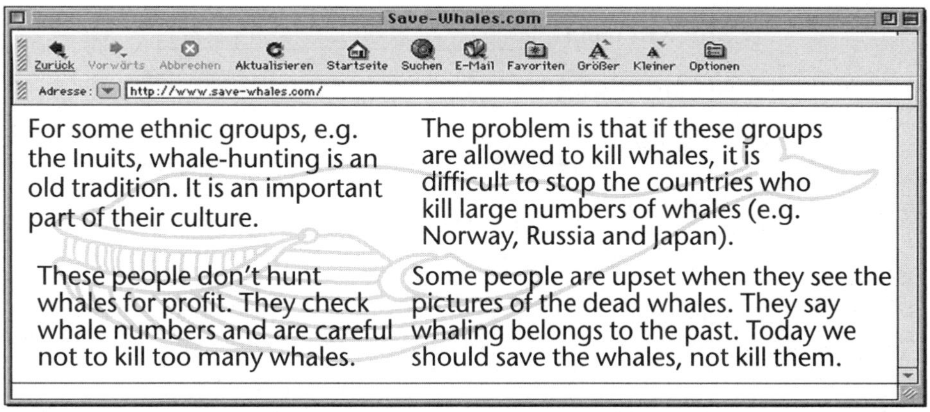
Save-Whales.com

Zurück Vorwärts Abbrechen Aktualisieren Startseite Suchen E-Mail Favoriten Größer Kleiner Optionen

Adresse: http://www.save-whales.com/

For some ethnic groups, e.g. the Inuits, whale-hunting is an old tradition. It is an important part of their culture.

These people don't hunt whales for profit. They check whale numbers and are careful not to kill too many whales.

The problem is that if these groups are allowed to kill whales, it is difficult to stop the countries who kill large numbers of whales (e.g. Norway, Russia and Japan).

Some people are upset when they see the pictures of the dead whales. They say whaling belongs to the past. Today we should save the whales, not kill them.

PARTNER Wir brauchen einige Punkte für den Walfang. Seit wann machen das die Inuit?

YOU Also hier steht, dass ______________________________

____

PARTNER Prima. Dürfen sie so viele Wale töten, wie sie wollen?

YOU Hier steht noch, dass ______________________________

____

____

PARTNER Gut. Jetzt brauchen wir einige Punkte gegen den Walfang.

YOU ______________________________

____

____

PARTNER Toll. Findest du noch einen Punkt?

YOU ______________________________

____

______________________________ p. 23/A3

7 ▶ Before Amy's trip

Look at what people said to Amy. Complete the sentences below.

1 Grandma invited me ______________________________ .

She will teach ______________________________ .

2 Dad told ______________________________ .

He expects ______________________________ .

3 Mom told ______________________________ .

She invited ______________________________ .

4 Glen asked ______________________________ .

5 My friend Judy asked ______________________________ . p. 24/A4

8 ▶ On a trip to Alaska

Imagine you are on a trip to Alaska. A German woman in your group wants to talk to a local woman. Tell the Alaskan woman what the German woman wants.

WOMAN Ich möchte, dass die alte Frau sich neben mich setzt.

YOU *She wants you to* ______________________________ .

WOMAN Ich möchte die Frau bitten, mir etwas über den kleinen Jungen zu erzählen.

YOU *She'd like* ______________________________

WOMAN Vielleicht würde sie mir etwas Inupiaq beibringen.

YOU ______________________________

WOMAN Ich möchte nicht, dass sie mich für unhöflich hält.

YOU ______________________________

WOMAN Ich möchte, dass sie mit mir zu Mittag isst.

YOU ______________________________

WOMAN Ich möchte gern, dass sie mir das Tanzen beibringt.

YOU ______________________________ . p. 24/A4

9 ▶ Nouns and verbs with the same form

a *Underline the words in the box that are both* verbs *and* nouns.

b *Now look at the words you have underlined and complete each of these sentences with one of them. (You might have to change the form of the word if it is a* verb.*)*

answer • arrive • call • celebrate • change • date • design • develop • dream • fish • joke • plant • report • ride • sleep • smile • stay • talk • visit • work

1 Glen has just written a *report* on his ____________ at Space Camp.

2 He is planning to ____________ rockets when he is older.

3 Tomorrow he is giving a ____________ about Space Camp at his school.

4 Glen always makes ____________ about Inuit traditions.

5 Amy always ____________ of going whaling.

6 When she was younger, her father taught her to ____________ and hunt.

7 Whaling was different. It was very hard ____________.

8 She'd like to move to Barrow, but it would be a big ____________ for her.

p. 25/A5

10 ▶ Plurals

Write down the plurals *of these words.*
One word in each group has a different kind of plural. *(Circle) it.*

wolf	____________	mouse	____________	photo	____________	fish	____________
family	____________	foot	____________	life	____________	city	____________
thief	____________	animal	____________	guy	____________	body	____________
knife	____________	tooth	____________	valley	____________	story	____________

p. 25/A5

11 ▶ A quick note

Complete the text with the correct prepositions from the box.

about • for • from • in • of • on • to • with

Dear Ann,

Just a quick note to say hi! Today wasn't a great day. There are some horrible kids in my class. If you're not a member ________ their gang, they make fun ________ you. They wait ________ me and my friends after school. My brother says he'll protect me ________ them – ha,ha! He's always arguing ________ me. (Mum says he's jealous ________ me.) Oh well, I can't waste time ________ those stupid kids. I prefer ________ think ________ the holidays. I'm going ________ vacation next week and I want to be ready ________ my trip. I'm real excited ________ it. Perhaps I'll meet someone nice and fall ________ love ________ him. I have to stop now and hunt ________ my bag.

Lots of love

p. 25/A5

WORKING WITH THE TEXT

12 ▶ Camping and hunting

Complete the network with words from the text on pages 30/31. Add more lines and words if you can.

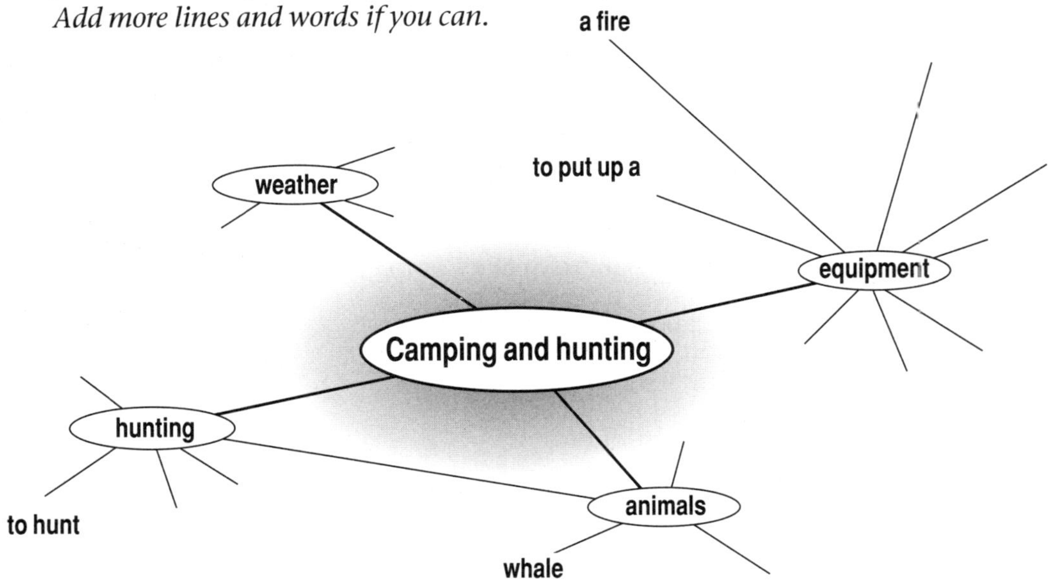

13 ▶ An interview with Lester Swenson

Imagine Lester is back in Barrow. How might he answer these questions?

Q Mr Swenson, you have just got back after a very exciting adventure. How did you feel when you woke up and your friend had left?

A *At first* ________________

But then ________________

____

____

Q And was it difficult to survive?

A *At first it was very* ________________

But then ________________

____

____

Q What would you say to your friend if you met him now?

A *If I met Henry,* ________________

____

Q One last question, Mr Swenson. Would you like to go camping again soon?

A ________________

____

pp. 30/31

Unit 2 NOW YOU CAN ...

14 ▶ ... be miserable in English

How do you say these things in English?

1 Ich bin erkältet.

____

2 Ich friere!

____

3 Ich sitze hier seit Stunden.

____

____

4 Ich glaube, die anderen machen sich über mich lustig.

____

____

5 Vielleicht wollen sie mir eine Lektion erteilen.

____

____

15 ▶ ... find the group words

What are they?

1 Supper is a *meal* .

2 A car is a ________________ .

3 A wolf is a ________________ .

4 A group of wolves is a ________________ .

5 The Inuits are native ________________ .

6 The USA is a ________________ .

7 Alaska is a ________________ .

8 Anchorage is a ________________ .

9 The Mississippi is a ________________ .

10 Denali is a ________________ and a ________________ .

16 ▶ ... write about the trip you'd like to go on

Where would you like to go? The USA? Alaska perhaps? Or Florida?
Or would you prefer somewhere different? Write about your dream trip.

- Who would you take with you? Why?
- What would/ wouldn't you do?
- What/Who would you take photos of?
- Who would you like to meet there?
- What souvenirs would you take home?

____

____

____

____

____

____

____

____

____

____

1 ▶ Getting to know your dictionary

a *Look at the* words at the top of the page *only. <u>Don't look at the rest of the page.</u>*
Do you think you'll find the words below on this page?

	yes	no
Hektar		
Hektik		
heftig		
heraus		
herab		

Look for the words on the page to check your answers.

b *Find words with* ***two*** *translations and* (circle) *them.*

c *Find a word with* ***three*** *translations and draw a* [box] *around it.*

d *Find a word with* ***more than three*** *translations. Underline it.*

heiraten 473 **heranwachsend**

heiraten get* married /get 'mærid/, marry* /'mæri/ **Sie werden im Juni heiraten.** They're getting married in June.

Get married ist gebräuchlicher als **marry: When are Sue and Ian getting married?** Wann heiraten Sue und Ian? **Are you getting married in church?** Heiratet ihr kirchlich? **They got married in 1992.** Sie haben 1992 geheiratet.

Heiratsantrag proposal /prə'pəʊzl/ **(jdm) einen Heiratsantrag machen** propose /prə'pəʊz/ (to sb)

heiser hoarse /hɔ:s/ (*Adv* hoarsely) **Er ist ganz heiser.** He's lost his voice.

heiß 1 hot* /hɒt/ **Die Teller sind heiß.** The plates are hot. **Heute ist es heiß.** It's hot today. **Mir ist heiß.** I'm hot.
2 (*Diskussion, Auseinandersetzung*) heated /'hi:tɪd/; (*Thema*) controversial /ˌkɒntrə'vɜ:ʃl/ **Das Gebiet ist heiß umkämpft.** The area is fiercely fought over.

heißen 1 be* called /kɔ:ld/ **Wie heißt Ihre Frau?** What's your wife called? **Ich heiße Walter.** My name is Walter.
2 mean* /mi:n/ (*nicht in ing-Formen*) **Was heißt „Tür" auf englisch?** What is the English for 'Tür'? **„Tür" heißt auf englisch „door".** The English for 'Tür' is 'door'. **Was soll das heißen?** What do you mean by that?
◆ **das heißt** that is to say … **es heißt, dass …** they say that … **jdn willkommen heißen** welcome /'welkəm/ sb

heiter (*Mensch*) cheerful /'tʃɪəfl/ (*Adv* cheerfully /'tʃɪəfəli/) (*Wetter*) fair /feə(r)/; (*Buch, Artikel*) light-hearted /ˌlaɪt 'hɑ:tɪd/
◆ **aus heiterem Himmel ⇨ Himmel**

heizen heat /hi:t/ **mit Strom heizen** use electricity for heating **Der Ofen heizt gut.** The heater is very efficient.

Heiz- Heizgerät heater /'hi:tə(r)/ **Heizkörper** radiator /'reɪdieɪtə(r)/

Heizung heating /'hi:tɪŋ/; (*Heizkörper*) radiator /'reɪdieɪtə(r)/ **eine Heizung einbauen** put in central heating

Hektar hectare /'hekteə(r)/ (*Abkürz* ha)

Hektik hectic rush **die Hektik des modernen Lebens** the hectic pace of modern life **die Hektik der Großstadt** the hectic life of the city

hektisch hectic /'hektɪk/ (*Adv* hectically /'hektɪkli/) frantic /'fræntɪk/ (*Adv* frantically /'fræntɪkli/) **eine hektische Suche** a frantic search

Held hero* /'hɪərəʊ/

heldenhaft heroic /hɪ'rəʊɪk/ (*Adv* heroically /hɪ'rəʊɪkli/)

Heldin heroine /'herəʊɪn/

helfen help /help/ **Könntest du mir beim Kochen helfen?** Could you help me with the cooking? **Ich half ihr, die Party zu organisieren.** I helped her to organize the party. **jdm über die Straße helfen** help sb across the road
◆ **es hilft nichts** it's no good **ich kann mir nicht helfen** I can't help it **Ich kann mir nicht helfen, aber ich mag ihn nicht.** I can't help not liking him. **jdm aus der Patsche helfen ⇨ Patsche; jdm ist nicht mehr zu helfen** sb is a hopeless case

Helfer(in) helper /'helpə(r)/

hell 1 light /laɪt/ **Im Sommer ist es früh hell.** In summer it's light early. **ein heller Raum** a light room
2 (*Licht, Lampe*) bright /braɪt/ (*Adv* brightly) **ein hell leuchtender Stern** a brightly shining star
3 (*Kleidung, Holz etc*) light-coloured /ˌlaɪt 'kʌləd/ (*AE* light-colored) **eine helle Hose** light-coloured trousers
4 (*Haut, Haare*) fair /feə(r)/
5 helles Bier lager /'lɑ:gə(r)/

hell- hellblau light blue **hellblond** very fair

Helligkeit brightness /'braɪtnəs/

hellsehen hellsehen können be* able to see into the future

hellwach wide awake /ˌwaɪd ə'weɪk/

Helm helmet /'helmɪt/

Hemd shirt /ʃɜ:t/

Hemisphäre hemisphere /'hemɪsfɪə(r)/

Hemmung inhibition /ˌɪnhɪ'bɪʃn/

hemmungslos without restraint /wɪˌðaʊt rɪ'streɪnt/

Henkel handle /'hændl/

Henne hen /hen/

her 1 etwas ist … her sth is* … ago /ə'gəʊ/ **Wie lange ist das jetzt her?** How long ago is it now? **Es ist vier Jahre her, dass wir uns das letzte Mal gesehen haben.** It's four years since we last saw each other.
2 hinter jdm/etwas her sein be* after sb/sth **Die Polizei ist schon lange hinter dem Verbrecher her.** The police have been after the criminal for a long time. **Sie ist nur hinter seinem Geld her.** She's only after his money.
3 von … her sein be* from … **Wo bist denn du her? Aus Köln?** Where are you from? Cologne?
◆ **her damit!** give me that! **Her mit dem Geld!** Hand over your money! **hin und her ⇨ hin; von … her ⇨ von**

herab down /daʊn/

herab- ☛ Siehe auch **hinab-, hinunter-, herunter-.**

herabsetzen 1 (*Standard*) lower /'ləʊə(r)/; (*Preis, Steuern, Geschwindigkeit*) reduce /rɪ'dju:s; *AE* rɪ'du:s/
2 (*schlecht machen*) belittle /bɪ'lɪtl/

Herabsetzung reduction /rɪ'dʌkʃn/

herangehen an etwas herangehen go* /gəʊ/ up to sth; (*an ein Problem etc*) approach /ə'prəʊtʃ/ sth

herankommen an jdn/etwas herankommen get* /get/ at sb/sth **Das Auto kam langsam heran.** The car approached slowly. **An das oberste Regal komme ich nicht heran.** I can't reach the top shelf. **Wie bist du an die Platte herangekommen?** How did you get hold of the record?

heranschleichen (sich) (an jdn/etwas) heranschleichen sneak /sni:k/ up (on sb/sth)

herantreten an jdn/etwas herantreten approach /ə'prəʊtʃ/ sb/sth

heranwachsend growing /'grəʊɪŋ/ **ein heranwach-**

from: *Das Oxford Schulwörterbuch* © Oxford University Press 1998

2 ▶ Symbols and abbreviations

Find these short forms and symbols on the dictionary page. Then match them to the correct long forms.

⇨	= adverb
jdm	= American English
jdn	= and so on
sb	= irregular form
Adv	= jemandem
AE	= jemanden
sth	= somebody
etc	= something
*	= go to another headword

3 ▶ Dictionary practice

Look up the German words and correct the mistakes.

1 We had a ~~hot~~ discussion. I got very angry.
hier: heiß = ____________

2 The weather was ~~cheerful~~ yesterday.
hier: heiter = ____________

3 You should ~~put down~~ your prices.
hier: herabsetzen = ____________

4 She has got ~~bright~~ hair. hier: hell = ____________

5 I can ~~get~~ the top shelf.
hier: herankommen = ____________

3 In Search of Colonial Virginia

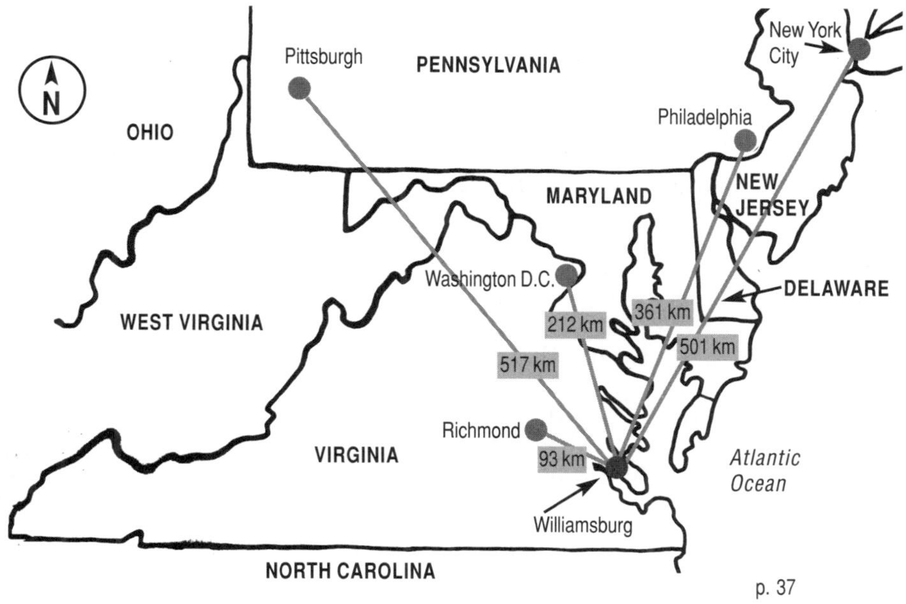

1 ▶ Williamsburg, Virginia

Look at the map.
Write a short paragraph about Virginia and Williamsburg in your exercise book.
Here are some ideas to help you:

part of U.S.A
near other states
near an ocean • capital
how far from other cities

p. 37

2 ▶ Visiting Colonial Williamsburg

Imagine you're a tourist in Colonial Williamsburg. You're standing in the street in this photo. Use the words and phrases in the boxes and write a paragraph.

- *Describe what you see/hear/feel.*
- *What are the people doing?*
- *What are the buildings like?*
- *What time of year is it?*
- *What's the weather like?*
- *Would you like to live here?*

buildings • coach[1] • clothes • crowds
hat • horse • people • shops
spring • summer • autumn • winter

busy • friendly • old • pretty
quiet • sunny • warm • ...

on the left/right
in the background/ foreground
Everybody looks/seems to be ...
I love the sound of ...

[1] coach [kəʊtʃ] *Kutsche*

What a place! I'm ______________________

____

____

____

____

____

____

____

______________________ p. 37

3 ▶ Who says what?

a *What do you think the people are saying? Match the sentences and the photos.*

a They're saying that they're getting fed up of marching. [5]

b She's saying that she likes selling things. [ ]

c He's saying that he loves her. [ ]

d They're saying that it's hot in their shop. [ ]

e She's saying that she's tired. [ ]

f They're saying that they like their house. [ ]

g He's saying that he works alone in his shop. [ ]

b *What exactly are they saying? Write down their words.*

a They're saying, *'We're getting fed up of marching.'*

b She's saying, '______________________________'

c He's saying, '________________'

d ____

e ____

f ____

g ____

p. 38/A2

4 ▶ Family trees

a *What does Mariah report to her mother?*

'I'm a descendant of a famous person.'

'His story is in an encyclopedia.'

'I'm going to check him out.'

'I want to write about him for the competition.'

Mom, Rebecca says that she's ______________________________

____

____

____

____

____

b *What does Rebecca report to her mother?*

'We have no famous ancestors.'

'Our family is boring.'

'I don't know enough about our family tree.'

'I'm going to invent a famous relative for the competition – Tina Turner!'

Mom, Mariah says that they ______________________________

____

____

____

____

____

p. 38/A2

5 ▶ A day in Colonial Williamsburg

Rebecca recorded some of the Colonial Williamsburg guides on her walkman and later she wrote down what she had learned. Read what the guides said and write Rebecca's paragraphs.

> Ladies and gentlemen, you've arrived in the 18th century – in 1776. You've changed your cars and buses into time machines and you've travelled back in time.

The first guide told us that we had arrived ______________________________

______________________________ *. He said* ______________________________

____

____

____

> You'll feel what it was really like to be alive in the past. You'll go into houses and shops. You'll speak to the people and you can ask lots of questions. You'll really learn a lot from them.

The next guide we met promised us that ______________________________

____

____

____

____

____

> Williamsburg is a famous town. John Smith met Pocahontas near here. Thomas Jefferson spent time in Williamsburg too. And you can even meet him in the streets. So watch out!

The third guide ______________________________

____

____

____

____

____

______________________________ p. 39/A3

6 ▶ Meeting somebody famous

The girls met Thomas Jefferson and asked him lots of questions. (Circle) *the six* time and place adverbs and adverbial phrases *in the paragraph, then write down the words Jefferson used.*

He told them that he had been born 33 years (before,) in 1743. He said he had lived there, in Virginia, where his father had been a plantation owner. He said he had read a lot of books the year before – in 1775 – and had helped to write the Declaration of Independence that year – in 1776. He told the girls that he wanted to work for independence then, and that he believed it would come the following year.

ago ______________ ______________

______________ ______________

______________ ______________

p. 39/A3

7 ▶ Reporting the meaning

Imagine you're on holiday in the USA. You're travelling around by bus with an American friend and you meet an older German tourist. He has lots of questions. Report the meaning of his questions to your friend – not all the details.

tip Remember! If you begin your report with a verb in the *present tense* (e.g. *He wants to know* … / *He's asking* … / *He wonders* …), there's ***no*** change in the tenses that follow. But if you decide to put the first verb in the *simple past* (e.g. *He said* … / *He asked* …), then the tenses will change.

TOURIST Ich will gern nach Richmond fahren, weiß aber nicht, ob ein Bus von Williamsburg nach Richmond fährt. Kannst du bitte danach fragen? Und wenn ja, wann er abfährt.

YOU *He says* ______________________________

____

TOURIST Vielleicht bleibe ich doch eine Nacht hier in Williamsburg. Die Stadt sieht ganz niedlich aus. Aber werde ich noch ein Zimmer finden? Ist es nicht zu spät? Wo soll ich suchen?

YOU ______________________________

____

TOURIST Ich habe seit Stunden nichts gegessen. Wo kann man hier so spät noch etwas zu essen bekommen?

YOU ______________________________

____

TOURIST Habt ihr auch Hunger? Ich lade euch ein. Was sagt ihr? Kommt doch mit. Mir nach.

YOU ______________________________

____

TOURIST Oh nein. Ich habe mein Geld im Bus vergessen. Was soll ich jetzt machen? Könnt ihr mir vielleicht etwas Geld leihen?

YOU ______________________________

______________________________ p. 40/A4

Just for fun

Can I become a hamburger with chips, please?

Of course, the German should say:
'Can I HAVE a hamburger with chips, please?'

8 ▶ Two worlds in Colonial Virginia

a *Look at the words and phrases. Make two lists – one for the world of the colonists, and one for the world of the slaves.*

16-hour days • black • easy life
house slaves • no rights
planters • plantation houses
property • rich • slave owners
slave quarters • white

colonists	slaves

b *Write a text and include as many of the words from* **a** *as possible.*

____
____
____
____
____
____
____ p. 41/A5

9 BLUE BOX get/become → blue box, p. 153

Complete these sentences. Use 'get' or 'become' and one of the words or phrases in the box. (Use each word once only.)

a good footballer • windy
angry • ill • old • a teacher
late • a taxi driver

1 You have to study if you want to ______________________.
2 I'm going to stop work and enjoy myself when I ______________________.
3 She's good at all sports. She has ______________________.
4 I've broken a mirror. Please don't ______________________.
5 There's a storm coming. It's going to ______________________.
6 I'll take a taxi if it ______________________.
7 Call a doctor if you ______________________.
8 When she leaves school she wants to ______________________.

▶▶▶ NOW YOU

Answer one of these questions. Write a paragraph in your exercise book.

- What do you want to do when you leave school?
- What do you do if it gets late and you can't get a bus home?
- When do you get angry?

WORKING WITH THE TEXT

10 ▶ People from history

a *The notes below are about people from the story on pages 46–48. Write the notes on the right cards.*

Adventure • attacked ships with slaves • black hat and coat • brought tobacco to England • *Dolphin* • English • home: Bristol • killed by slaves • killed in 1718 killed in 1728 • left ship at Point Comfort • long beard • married with children pirate • *Ranger* • returned with skull • sent to stop Blackbeard • shot Teach in 1718 wild eyes / tall

Captain Keene	Edward Teach	Captain Maynard

b *Choose one of the men and, with the help of the notes, write a short paragraph about him in your exercise book.*

11 ▶ In the Raleigh Tavern

You are John, the owner of the tavern, or Mary, the waitress. Some days later you tell a friend what happened that evening in 1728 and the next morning. Describe what happened, what you saw and what you heard. What about the next morning? How did the two men feel? What did they think?

A strange thing happened a few days ago. It was a normal evening and Thomas and George were talking quietly.

The door opened

pp. 46–48

Unit 3 NOW YOU CAN ...

12 ▶ ... visit a museum in English

How do you say these things in English?

1 Ist diese Karte gültig für den ganzen Tag?

____

____

____

2 Hier steht, dass der Besitzer noch lebt.

____

____

____

3 Diese Geschichte ist unglaublich.

____

____

4 Wirf einen Blick hierauf!

____

____

5 Nicht einschlafen!

____

13 ▶ ... find the fourth word

1 hello	–	greeting	3 hot	–	warm	5 warn	–	warning
chair	–	__________	beautiful	–	__________	die	–	__________
2 come	–	go	4 accident	–	disaster	6 left	–	right
pick up	–	__________	fear	–	__________	foreground	–	__________
								__________

14 ▶ ... write about a visit to a museum

Choose **a** *or* **b**.

a *Describe a museum you know. Did you enjoy your visit? What did you think was good about the museum? What was not so good? How could they make the museum more interesting for visitors?*

b *It is the year 2100. You have just visited a living-history museum that shows the way people lived in 2000. Write about what you saw, heard and felt. What were the people doing, saying and thinking?*

____

____

____

____

____

____

____

____

____

____

____

Revision USA Facts (Units 1–3)

You already know a lot about the USA. Probably more than you think!
Try this quiz and test yourself. (Don't look in your pupil's book before you do the quiz.) When you've finished, check your answers. (Look at Units 1–3 of your pupil's book and look at the maps, too.)

1 An ATV is:

- a ☐ a vehicle
- b ☐ a TV programme
- c ☐ a movie studio

2 Chicago airport is called:

- a ☐ O'Hare
- b ☐ La Guardia
- c ☐ Heathrow

3 In Alaska you can't find wild …

- a ☐ bears
- b ☐ moose
- c ☐ crocodiles

4 In British English, the AE word 'neat' is:

- a ☐ tidy
- b ☐ great
- c ☐ small

5 It's nine o'clock in Florida.
In Virginia it is:

- a ☐ an hour earlier
- b ☐ two hours later
- c ☐ the same time

6 One of these places is not in Virginia:

- a ☐ Richmond
- b ☐ Washington D.C.
- c ☐ Williamsburg

7 One of these states is *not* a neighbour of Virginia:

- a ☐ Maryland
- b ☐ North Carolina
- c ☐ South Carolina

8 Tacos are:

- a ☐ wild dogs
- b ☐ Mexican food
- c ☐ rappers

9 The Alaskan summer is special because:

- a ☐ it's as cold as a European winter
- b ☐ it doesn't get dark at night
- c ☐ the sun never shines

10 The capital of Alaska is:

- a ☐ Anchorage
- b ☐ Juneau
- c ☐ Barrow

11 The capital of Florida is:

a ☐ Tallahassee
b ☐ Miami
c ☐ Jacksonville

12 The capital of the USA is:

a ☐ New York
b ☐ Washington D.C
c ☐ Los Angeles

13 The German translation for 'high school' is:

a ☐ Hochschule
b ☐ Universität
c ☐ Gesamtschule

14 The highest mountain in North America is:

a ☐ Denali
b ☐ Mount McKinley
c ☐ Mount St. Helen's

15 The Inuits have been in Alaska for:

a) ☐ about 800 years
b) ☐ about 8,000 years
c) ☐ about 80,000 years

16 The most important date in Williamsburg's history was:

a ☐ 1699
b ☐ 1700
c ☐ 1704

17 The odd one out is:

a ☐ Thomas Jefferson
b ☐ George Washington
c ☐ Robert 'King' Carter

18 The population of the USA is:

a ☐ about 27 million
b ☐ about 270 million
c ☐ about 720 million

19 The US state that is known as the 'Sunshine State' is:

a ☐ Florida
b ☐ California
c ☐ Maryland

20 They (or their ancestors) came from South America to live in the USA:

a ☐ Hispanics
b ☐ Mexicans
c ☐ Spaniards

21 They lived in 'fear and terror':

a ☐ pirates
b ☐ planters
c ☐ slaves

22 The national bird of the USA is:

a ☐

b ☐

c ☐

4 New York – Gateway to America

1 ▶ Immigrants

a *Complete this network about immigrants.*

Immigrants

They all hope for …
- a b______r life
- find a place to l____e

They leave their own countries because of …
- p______________n
- h_________r
- p_________y

When they arrive they have to …
- find w____k
- go through the i______________n process
- learn a new l___________ge

On the journey to the new country they feel …
- s__d
- wo______d
- ex______d
- ner______s

b *Complete these tables.*

noun	adjective
danger	*dangerous*
religion	______
poverty	______
hunger	______
thirst	______
freedom	______

noun	verb
immigration	______
hope	______
decision	______
life	______

pp. 50/51

2 The journey to America

Complete the text. Some of the words are missing, but the first letter is there.

Many immigrants to America *didn't* want to leave their own c______________ . They left because of poverty or p_________________ . The journey t_ America was exciting f_____some people. But m_______ felt sad or n__________ . When people decided to l_______ home, they had to say g____________ to their families and f__________ and sometimes they d_________ see them again. Life in America w____________ easy for immigrants. Many of t_______ didn't know any E___________ . They didn't have much m_________ and they only brought a f______ things with them from h_________ . But they were all r_________ to work and they h_________ for a better l______ in a free country.

pp. 50/51

3 **REVISION** Before Daniel's bar mitzvah

Report what they said. Use indirect speech.

1 Mrs Schwarz told Daniel *she had found* ______.

2 Mrs Schwarz asked Daniel ______.

3 Daniel told her ______.

4 She wanted to know why ______.

5 Daniel asked his mother ______.

6 Daniel explained ______.

______

4 ▶ What do you think?

Add the *only where you need it.*

1 a 'What do you think of ______ rap music?'

b 'I liked ______ programme about rap last night.'

2 a 'Look at ______ dolphins. Aren't they great?'

b 'Do you know that ______ dolphins are in great danger?

3 a 'I believe that we must stop ______ pollution at once.'

b 'Isn't ______ pollution of the river terrible?'

4 a 'I love ______ spaghetti.'

b '______ spaghetti my dad makes is fantastic.'

p. 52/A2

5 ▶ What do you enjoy?

Add the *where you need the* article.

1 'Do you like reading _____ computer magazines?'

– 'Sometimes. There were some interesting articles in _____ last magazine I read.'

2 'Did you watch _____ film *The Beach* on TV last night?'

– 'No, I don't like watching _____ films like that.'

3 'My brother loves watching _____ car races.'

– 'Did he watch _____ race at Monte Carlo yesterday?'

4 'I don't like _____ hot weather.'

– 'Really? I love going on holiday to _____ hot places.'

5 'Have you ever dreamed of making _____ music?'

– 'Yes, I have. I really love _____ music of the sixties.'

6 'My mother enjoys going to _____ museums very much.'

– 'My mother enjoys going to _____ concerts most of all.'

p. 52/A2

Just for fun

Why does the Statue of Liberty stand in New York Harbor?
– Because it can't sit down.

6 ▶ REVISION Dreams

Sometimes Josh thinks about his dream trip. Complete the sentences. Use the correct form of the verbs.

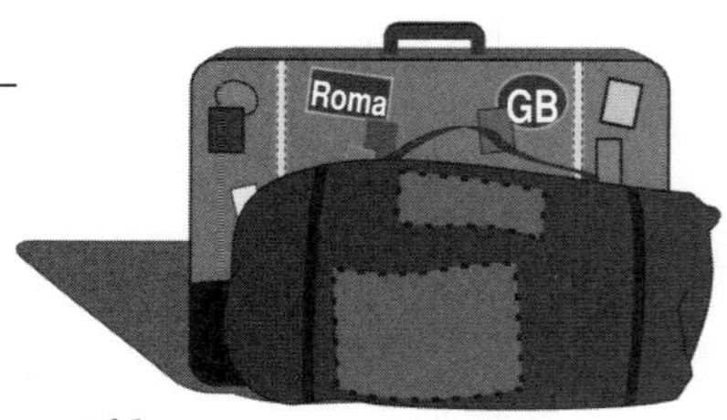

1 If I (have) *had* _____ lots of money, I (go) _____________ on my dream trip.

2 If I (can) _________________ go wherever I wanted,

I (choose) ____________________ Europe.

3 I (take) ________________ my best friend Daniel with me if he

(want) ________________ to come.

4 If he (not, want) __________________ to come, I (travel) __________________ alone.

5 We (not, have) _____________________ a problem with the language if we

(go) _____________ to England.

6 But if we (visit) ________________ Germany or France,

I (not, understand) ______________________________ a word of the language.

▶▶▶ NOW YOU

Complete these sentences. Use your own ideas.
(They can be funny.)

1 If I could go anywhere in the world … ______________________________

2 My life would be perfect if … ______________________________

3 I'd hate it if … ______________________________

4 If my best friend stole my boy/girlfriend … ______________________________

5 If I had to move to another country … ______________________________

7 ▶ Help the tourist

You're visiting Berlin when you meet a British tourist. Complete the conversation.

TOURIST Excuse me. Can you tell me how to get to the Reichstag?

YOU Sorry, I'm not from Berlin. But I'll ask. *(To bus driver:)* Entschuldigen Sie, die Dame möchte zum Reichstag. ______

DRIVER Sag ihr, sie soll den 100-er Bus nehmen.

YOU You ______.

DRIVER Gehen Sie am Bahnhof vorbei. Die Bushaltestelle ist auf der anderen Straßenseite.

YOU ______

______

DRIVER Der nächste Bus kommt aber erst in 10 Minuten. Nehmen Sie doch ein Taxi.

YOU ______

______

TOURIST Actually, I prefer travelling by bus. You see more – and meet nice people.

YOU ______

______

TOURIST Please thank the bus driver for me and tell him he has helped me a lot. And thank you, too.

YOU ______

p. 53/A3
+ p.122

8 BLUE BOX British and American English → blue box, p. 156

Sometimes Americans use words that are different in British English. How does the English girl 'translate' Josh's AE into BE?

1 Are you having a nice *vacation?* ... *holiday.*

2 The Bronx is *real neat.* ... ______.

3 It's hot here from June *through* September. ... June ______ September.

4 It isn't so hot here in the *fall.* ... the ______.

5 The *sidewalks* are always busy. ... the ______.

6 But it's fun, I *guess.* ... ______.

7 Want to come to a *movie?* ... a ______.

8 I know a great *movie theater* on Fifth Avenue. ... a ______.

9 We can take the *subway.* ... the ______.

10 But I have to go back to my *apartment* first. ... his ______.

11 We live on the *first floor.* ... the ______.

12 So we don't have to take the *elevator.* ... the ______.

p. 53/A3

9 ▶ What really happened?

Tick the right picture.

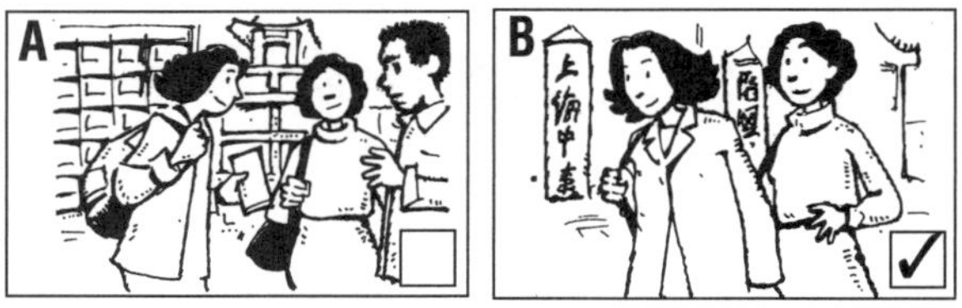

1 If the girls had asked Josh, he would have gone to Chinatown with them.

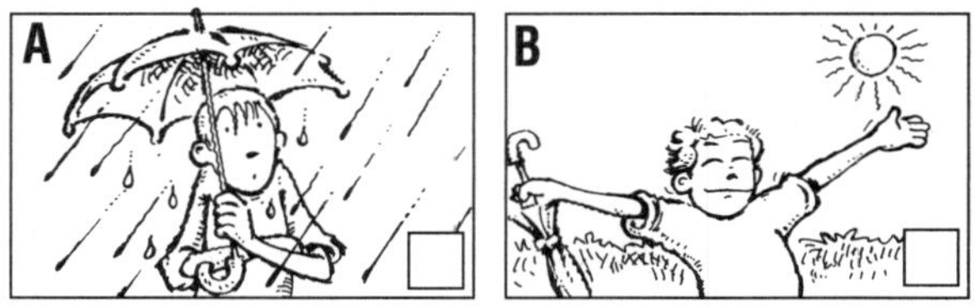

2 If it hadn't rained, I wouldn't have got wet.

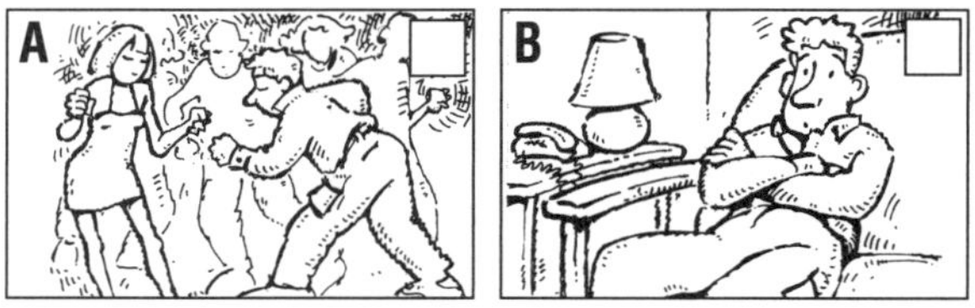

3 If my friend had called, I would have gone out last night.

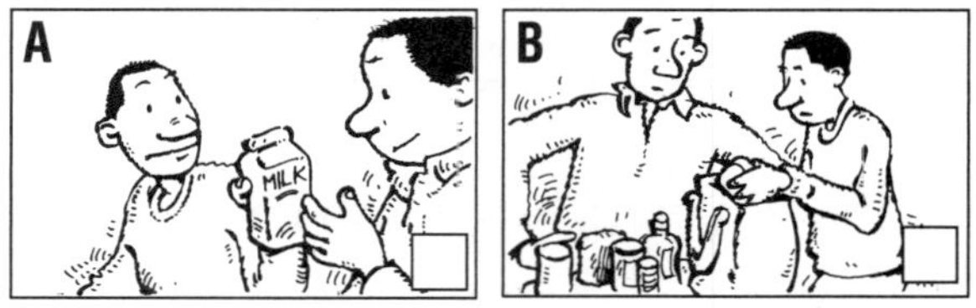

4 If I had forgotten the milk, Dad would have been fed up.

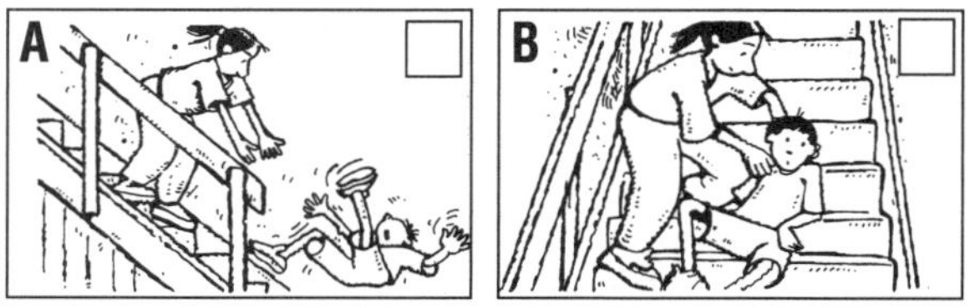

5 If I hadn't caught my brother, he would have hurt himself.

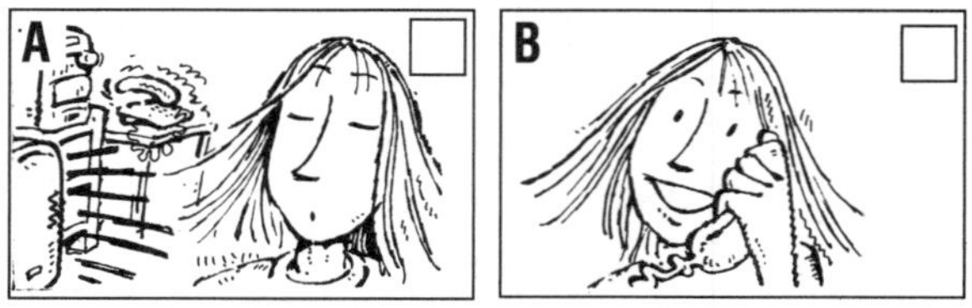

6 If the music hadn't been so loud, I would have heard the phone.

p.54/A4

10 ▶ What would have happened?

Complete these sentences.

1 I didn't win the race. I didn't start my training early enough.

If I had started my training early enough, I *would have* ______________________.

2 I've lost my bicycle key. I didn't put it in my pocket.

If I had put my bicycle key in my pocket, I ______________________.

3 I didn't get up on time. I didn't catch the bus.

If I had got up on time, I ______________________.

4 I didn't shout. The car didn't stop.

______________________.

5 I didn't phone Mum. She worried.

______________________.

6 I had trouble with my best friend. We didn't go to the cinema.

______________________.

____

▶▶▶ NOW YOU

What if these things had happened ***today****? Use your imagination.*
Choose one of these sentences. Write a paragraph in your exercise book.

a If you had woken up this morning in the year 1955.
b If a spaceship had landed in your town.
c If you had met your favourite pop-star in the street.
d If someone had given you lots of money.

p. 54/A4

WORKING WITH THE TEXT

11 ▶ A Knight in New York

Here are twelve notes about the story on pages 59–62. Eight of them are main points, but four of them aren't really important.

a *Decide which order the notes are in – what happened first, second, etc.
Write the numbers 1–12 in the circles on the notes.*

b *Decide which notes are important and put a tick in the boxes on eight of the notes.*

(1) Ray – in NY – first time – visit cousin ☑	( ) get out of elevator – Lower East Side – meet Jim ☐	( ) different places – city – collect numbers ☐	( ) Central Park – find horses – heard prices – wrote 33 ☐
( ) Ray – write down 1st digit – 6 clues ☐	( ) Ray – party – Josie – phone number – challenge instead ☐	( ) skyscrapers huge – people colourfully dressed – Ray feel at home ☐	( ) next day – Ray and Maria – look for more numbers ☐
( ) Ray and Maria – great day together – forget challenge ☐	( ) Maria Gomez – help Ray – map ☐	( ) Ray phone – Josie not there – 2nd part of challenge ☐	( ) Josie phone – want to meet Ray – not interested ☐

c *Use the important notes and write a summary of the story.*

Ray is in New York for the first time ____________________

____

____

____

____

____

____

____

____

____

____

12 ▶ ... discuss your day out in English

1 Sage, dass du den Central Park sehen möchtest.

2 Sage, dass es dir egal ist und schlage vor, mit dem Bus zu fahren.

3 Sage, dass es mit der U-Bahn schneller geht.

4 Sage, dass ihr nachher zum Broadway fahren könntet.

5 Sage, dass du lieber zu Macy's zum Einkaufen fahren würdest.

13 ▶ ... find another name for New York

Complete the puzzle to find out another name for New York.

1 The borough north of Manhattan.
2 Brooklyn Bridge goes across it.
3 The name of an airport and a high school.
4 Here you can buy whatever you want to.
5 The biggest park in New York.
6 The ... State Building.
7 This borough has the largest population.
8 The most exciting square in New York.

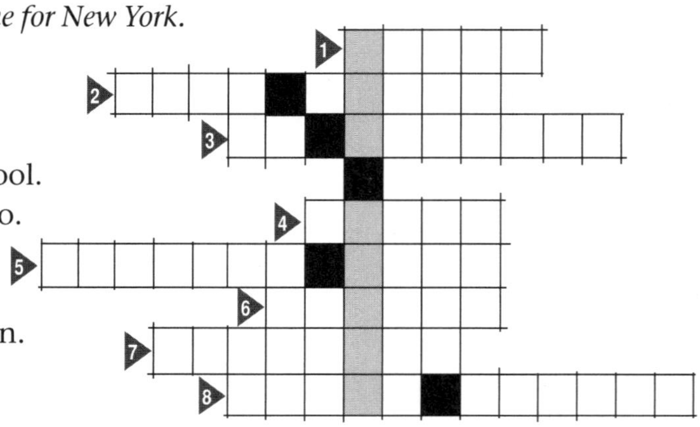

14 ▶ ... write about a family celebration

Write about a special family party.

What kind of party was it?
Where was it?
Who came?
Did everybody wear special clothes?
Did someone make a speech?
Was it boring or funny?
Was there music?
Did people dance?
Did you enjoy it?

1 ▶ Getting to know your dictionary

a *Find the short forms of these grammar words on the page.*

Adjektiv: ____________

Adverb: ____________

Pronomen: ____________

Objekt: ____________

b *Find two grammar words that haven't got short forms.*

____

____

c *Look at the phonetic symbols. Find one word for each symbol.*

ɪ *nibble*

a ____________

iː ____________

θ ____________

əʊ ____________

d *Find one English word with two German meanings.*

________ = 1 ____________

2 ____________

e *What's the* adverb *form of these adjectives?*

She asked me (nice) __________.

They played (noisy) __________.

f *Find these short forms on the page. What do they mean?*

BE

____

umgs

____

nibble 186 **none**

wonder what will happen next. Ich frage mich, was als Nächstes passieren wird. **It was years until I next saw her.** Bis ich sie das nächste Mal sah, vergingen Jahre.
▲ **ˌnext-ˈbest** *Adj* nächstbeste(r,s)

nibble /ˈnɪbl/ *Verb* knabbern

nice /naɪs/ *Adj* **1** angenehm, schön, gut **Have a nice day!** Einen schönen Tag! **You look very nice today.** Du siehst heute sehr hübsch aus. **This doesn't taste very nice.** Das schmeckt nicht besonders gut.
2 nett
◆ **nice and …** (*umgs*) schön … **It's nice and warm by the fire.** Es ist schön warm am Kamin.

nicely /ˈnaɪsli/ *Adv* **1** nett **You can have a biscuit if you ask nicely.** Du bekommst einen Keks, wenn du nett fragst.
2 (*umgs*) sehr gut **This flat will suit us nicely.** Diese Wohnung wird uns vollauf genügen.

nick /nɪk/ *Verb + Obj* (*BE*) (*Slang*) **1** klauen
2 nick sb (for sth) jdn (für etwas) einsperren

nickel /ˈnɪkl/ *Nomen* **1** Nickel
2 Fünfcentstück

nickname /ˈnɪkneɪm/ *Nomen* Spitzname

nicotine /ˈnɪkətiːn/ *Nomen* Nikotin

niece /niːs/ *Nomen* Nichte

night /naɪt/ *Nomen* **1** Nacht **Why don't you stay the night?** Willst du nicht über Nacht bleiben? **Owls come out at night.** Eulen werden nachts munter.
2 Abend **Let's go out on Saturday night.** Lass uns Samstagabend ausgehen. **8 o'clock at night** 8 Uhr abends **I tried to phone Nigel last night.** Ich habe gestern Abend versucht, Nigel anzurufen.
◆ **have an early/a late night** früh/spät ins Bett gehen **good night** gute Nacht
▲ **ˈnightdress** *Nomen* Nachthemd **ˈnight school** *Nomen* Abendschule **ˈnight-time** *Nomen, kein Plural* Nacht

nightie /ˈnaɪti/ *Nomen* (*umgs*) Nachthemd

nightly /ˈnaɪtli/ **1** *Adj* allabendlich, allnächtlich
2 *Adv* jeden Abend, jede Nacht

nightmare … traum

ninth[1] /naɪnθ/ *Pronom, Adj* neunte(r,s) ☛ Anwendungsbeispiele für Zahlwörter stehen unter **sechste(r,s)**.

ninth[2] /naɪnθ/ *Pronom, Nomen* Neuntel

nip /nɪp/ *Verb* (nipping, nipped, nipped) **1** zwicken
2 *ohne Obj* (*umgs*) flitzen **She nipped round to the shop.** Sie ging kurz zum Laden.

nitrate /ˈnaɪtreɪt/ *Nomen* Nitrat

nitrogen /ˈnaɪtrədʒən/ *Nomen* Stickstoff

no[1] /nəʊ/ *Adj* kein **No two days are the same.** Kein Tag ist wie der andere. **He's no friend of mine.** Er ist kein Freund von mir. **No smoking.** Rauchen verboten.
◆ **no way** (*umgs*) auf keinen Fall
▲ **ˈno one** *Pronom* niemand, keiner **No one else was there.** Sonst war niemand da.

no[2] /nəʊ/ *Adv* nicht **Alice is feeling no better this morning.** Alice fühlt sich heute früh nicht besser. **no later than 31st July** bis spätestens 31. Juli

no[3] /nəʊ/ *Ausruf* nein ☛ Hinweis bei **nein**.

nobility /nəʊˈbɪləti/ *Nomen* Adel

noble[1] /ˈnəʊbl/ *Adj* **1** edel, hochherzig
2 adlig

noble[2] /ˈnəʊbl/ *Nomen* Adlige

nobly /ˈnəʊbli/ *Adv* edelmütig

nobody /ˈnəʊbədi/ *Pronom* niemand, keiner **He screamed but nobody came to help him.** Er schrie, aber niemand kam ihm zu Hilfe. **There was nobody at home.** Keiner war zu Hause.

nocturnal /nɒkˈtɜːnl/ *Adj* **1** nächtlich
2 (*Tiere*) Nacht-

nod[1] /nɒd/ *Verb* (nodding, nodded, nodded) nicken **Nod your head if you understand me.** Nicken Sie mit dem Kopf, wenn Sie mich verstehen.

nod[2] /nɒd/ *Nomen* Nicken

noise /nɔɪz/ *Nomen* Geräusch, Lärm **Try not to make a noise.** Bemüh dich, keinen Lärm zu machen. **Why is the engine making so much noise?** Warum ist der Motor so laut?

noisy /ˈnɔɪzi/ *Adj* (**noisier, noisiest**) (*Adv* **noisily**) lärmend, laut ☛ Hinweis bei **laut**.

nominate …

from: *Das Oxford Schulwörterbuch* © Oxford University Press 1998

2 ▶ Dictionary practice

Use your own dictionary and find the best German translation for the underlined words.

Fiorello Henry LaGuardia was a well-known[1] American politician in the 1930s and 1940s. He was raised[2] in Arizona, but moved to Italy as a young man. When he returned to the US he worked temporarily[3] on Ellis Island as an interpreter[4]. Later he entered politics[5] and in 1933 he was elected[6] mayor of New York City. He was very popular and for a long time he was the host[7] of his own radio programme. He did lots of good things for New York. For example, in 1936 he founded[8] the LaGuardia High School of Music and Art. Today New York's main airport is named after him[9].

1 ____________ 7 ____________

2 ____________ 8 ____________

3 ____________ 9 ____________

4 ____________ ____________

5 ____________

6 ____________

5 Nebraska – the Middle of Nowhere?

1 ▶ The big school crossword puzzle

Complete this puzzle.

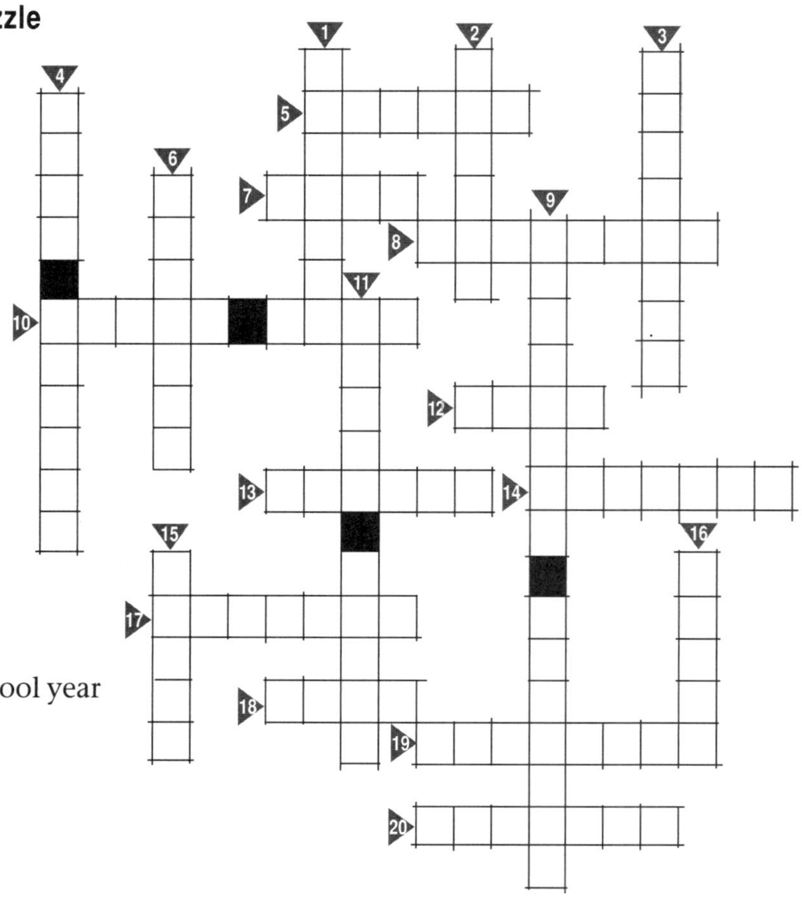

Across

5 The number of Nancy's ... is 142.
7 At school, there are three a year.
8 You need one if you want to surf the Internet.
10 The time for your homework at school
12 A short test
13 A place where people go to learn
14 A grade between 'very good' and 'poor'
17 A room or building for books
18 A big test at the end of the school year
19 An AE word for 'timetable'
20 A person who gives lessons

Down

1 A part of Maths
2 An AE word for 'lesson'
3 English, Maths, Biology, PE, etc.
4 School in the USA for classes 7–12
6 Another word for 'pupil'
9 Physics, Chemistry and Biology
11 The time for a meal at school
15 A group of pupils at school
16 An AE word for 'mark'

pp. 64/65

2 ▶ Nebraska – where is it?

Look at this map of Nebraska and write a short paragraph about the state in your exercise book.

Some ideas
- where in USA
- neighbours
- cities and towns
- capital
- rivers

p. 66/A1

3 ▶ What kind of a person is Nancy?

We know a bit about Nancy already, and we can guess more about her, too.
Use gerunds *to complete the sentences about her. Look at the photos on pages 64/65 of your pupil's book and the ideas in the box.*

be with her boyfriend
do her school work
eat in the school cafeteria • go to games
live in a bigger town • live in Sutton
play in the school band • remember facts
think of him

1 We know Nancy has a good memory. She's usually good at *remembering facts.*

2 We know she loves ______________________________ .

3 She keeps ____________________ .

4 It looks like Nancy enjoys __________________ . Look at photo F.

5 Her hobby is probably ________________________________. Look at photo E.

6 I don't think she likes ___________________________________. Look at her face in photo D!

7 I bet she's good at _________________________ . Look at photo G.

8 She probably hates ___________________. It's so boring there.

9 I'm sure she dreams of ___________________________ – somewhere like Lincoln or even L.A.

▶▶▶ NOW YOU

What kind of person are you? Write a paragraph about yourself. Use phrases like:

I like ... / I love ... / I worry about ... / I'm looking forward to ... / I hate ... /
I'm good at ... / I often think about ... / I dream of ... / I'm terrible at ... / I believe in ...

____
____
____
____
____
____
____

p. 66/A1

4 ▶ An e-mail from L.A.

Nancy's cousin Steve is from L.A. He has decided to move to the country for a year for a new experience.
Write his e-mail to Nancy in your exercise book. In each sentence, you should use a gerund *or a* to-infinitive.

hate – live city
decide – move – to country – for a year
would like – come – Sutton
mention – leave home – to parents – say OK
plan – arrive – August
look forward – go – your school
hope – be – your class
won't miss – live – city

p. 66/A1

5 ▶ Steve's new life

a *Some time later Steve is living in Sutton. Complete this e-mail from him to an old friend in L.A. Use the correct form of the verbs in the box.*

breathe • enjoy • leave • live • sell
sit • spend • take

Middle of nowhere

From...
To... Tess
Cc...
Subject: Middle of nowhere

Dear Tess,
Here I am in Nebraska. After ________ all my life in the city, I finally moved to the country in August. Before ________ L.A., I sold lots of things, my sports car, my stereo, my city clothes. I wanted to start a new life without ________ any of my city things with me. And I thought by ________ all those things I would become a happier person. Instead of ________ for hours in L.A. traffic and ________ all day in polluted air, I thought I would live in a quiet, clean environment. Well, Tess, it is _too_ quiet round here – and I spend all my time in a car. After ________ two months in the country, I'm ready to come back to L.A. again. See you next week. Steve.

b *Write what Steve did after sending the e-mail. Use* gerunds.

after – spend – eight weeks – Sutton – Steve – return – L.A.

on – arrive home – phone – old friend – organize – party

before – meet – friends – buy – new clothes

instead – buy – car – buy – bicycle

____
____
____
____
____
____
____

p. 67/A3

6 ▶ BLUE BOX False friends → blue box, p. 160

Choose the right word for each sentence and (circle) it.

1 Excuse me, please. Where's the next / nearest post office?
2 After studying for years, he became / got a teacher at last.
3 Would you like a piece of biscuit / cake ?
4 I'll meet you in the floor / hall in ten minutes.
5 I got a good mark / note for English.
6 I wrote a note / notice to my friend in class.
7 Dr Brown will be here soon. Please take a place / seat for a minute.
8 The children were very brave / good . They helped me with the cooking.
9 They've built a new bright / wide road. It'll take more traffic.
10 I'd like a plate of chips / crisps with my meal, please.

7 ▶ MADD – facts about alcohol in the USA

Complete the facts about young people and alcohol with the passive *of the verbs.*

Over 40% of all 16–20 year olds who died in 1994 (kill) ______________ in car crashes. Each year more money (spend) __________ on alcohol than on tea, milk, juice and books together. During a typical weekend in 1999, one teenager (kill) ______________ each hour. On weekend nights in 1994, 72% of all drivers who (hurt) ______________ very badly were under 25 years old. Alcohol (drink) ___________ by 40% of students who have problems at school. For these reasons MADD (found) ________________ in 1980 in the USA. The members feel that cars (drive) _____________ too fast. They say that young people (not, warn) ________________ enough about the dangers of drinking and driving.

▶▶▶ NOW YOU

You are at a party with a friend. You've missed the last bus home and it's too far to walk. An older boy/girl offers to take you both home in his/her car. Your friend wants to accept, but you saw the older boy/girl drink alcohol at the party. Write the conversation between the three of you in your exercise book. (You might like to act it out in front of the class with two classmates.)

p. 67/A4

8 ▶ A friend of mine

Complete the sentences. Use 'of'.

1 Lily is one of my friends. She's a great *friend* ______________________________.
2 This is one of my books. It's a favourite ______________________________.
3 Is Tom one of your cousins? Or is he a friend ______________________________?
4 Are these Annie's kids? – Yes, they're all ______________________________.
5 Meet, Jim, one of our uncles. He's an American ______________________________.
6 Are the Smiths your neighbours? – Yes, and they're good friends ________________.
7 Is that one of the Smiths' cars ? – Yes, it's a new ______________________________.

p. 68/A5

9 ▶ A 'School and Home Contract'

Translate this message from a school notice board in your exercise book.

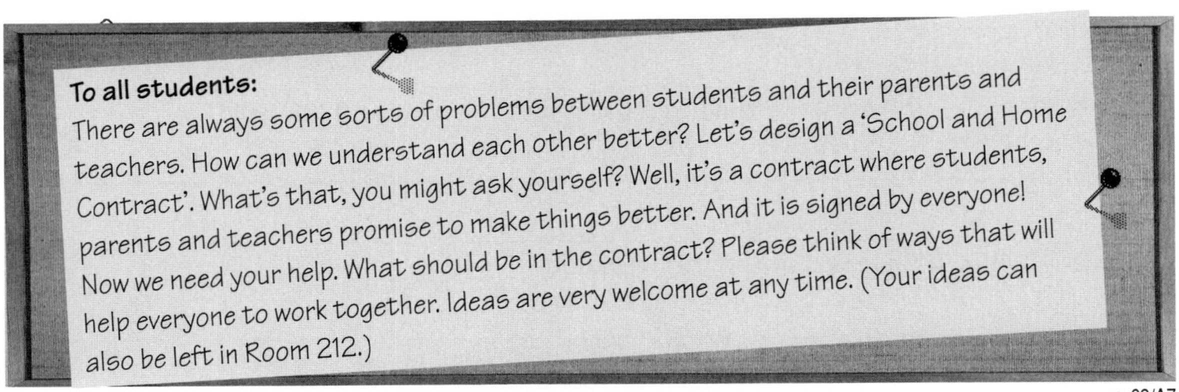

To all students:
There are always some sorts of problems between students and their parents and teachers. How can we understand each other better? Let's design a 'School and Home Contract'. What's that, you might ask yourself? Well, it's a contract where students, parents and teachers promise to make things better. And it is signed by everyone! Now we need your help. What should be in the contract? Please think of ways that will help everyone to work together. Ideas are very welcome at any time. (Your ideas can also be left in Room 212.)

p. 69/A7

WORKING WITH THE TEXT

10 ▶ An A – Z of describing people

a *For each letter of the alphabet, find an* adjective *that describes people (how they look, what they are like). You can find some on pages 74/75.*

a angry ______
b ______
c ______
d ______
e ______
f ______
G ______
h ______
i ______
j ______
K ______
l ______
m ______
N ______
o ______
p ______
Q ______
R ______
S ______
T ______
u ______
V ______
w ______
x se _ y ______
Y ______
z la _ y ______

b *Describe Laura or Mike in a paragraph in your exercise-book.*

11 ▶ Laura and Mike talk

When Laura and Mike leave the library at the end of the scene, they meet at the door. The situation has embarrassed them both a little. How do you think the dialogue might go? Write what you think Laura says.

MIKE Listen, Laura, I need to talk to you. Can we go somewhere quiet for a few minutes?

LAURA ______

MIKE Do you know that people are talking about us? Do you know what they are saying?

LAURA ______

MIKE It's OK to be just good friends, isn't it?

LAURA ______

MIKE People say that we're too different. You're so pretty and I'm, well …

LAURA ______

MIKE Well, what are you doing this weekend?

LAURA ______

p. 74/75

12 ▶ ... talk about a date

How do you say these things in English?

1 Sage, dass du eine Verabredung mit Tina/Tino hast.

____

2 Sage, dass du sie/ihn abholen wirst.

____

3 Sage, dass ihr vereinbart habt, ins Kino zu gehen.

____

4 Sage, dass du dich beeilen musst, sonst kommst du zu spät.

____

5 Frage, was los ist.

____

6 Sage, dass du gerade gemerkt hast, dass du die Adresse vergessen hast.

____

13 ▶ ... find the preposition

What preposition can go with all the words or phrases in each group?

lie, react, pay attention, reply	________
get along, mad, connect, make a date	________
separate, protect, judge, accept a ride	________
care, talk, comment, worry	________
impression, instead, typical, memory	________

14 ▶ ... write about school

What do you like about American high schools? What do you like better at your German school?

Write about
- lessons and subjects
- homework
- where you eat
- activities at school
- classroom
- timetable
- lockers
- how you get to school
- ...

____

6 Dreamland California

1 ▶ Things you can do in a National Park

Use verbs to complete the text.

You can do so many things in America's National Parks.

__________ a mountain,

_______ a walk in a deep canyon,

_______ a horse,

_________ a bridge over a wild river,

_______ photos of giant trees,

__________ a tent in a beautiful camp-site,

_____ for a bike ride along a lovely valley.

Feel tired? __________ a video in a visitor center!

Whatever you do, you'll _________ a fantastic time. We promise!

▶▶▶ NOW YOU

Make a list of the kind of things you can do around your area. Design a poster for tourists.

p. 80/A1

2 ▶ 50 miles an hour

Look at the signs. Then complete the sentences with phrases like 50 miles an hour, $ 10 a bottle, *etc.*

1 The wine costs *$10 a bottle* ____________.
2 The speed limit is ____________.
3 The restaurant is open ____________.
4 The orange juice costs ____________.
5 The tea costs ____________.
6 The adventure club meets ____________.
7 There's a talk ____________.
8 There's a video ____________.

▶▶▶ NOW YOU

Answer the questions. Use phrases like: once a week, two hours a day, *etc.*

How often do you get homework? ____________

How often do you do sport? ____________

How much TV do you watch? ____________

How much does cola cost in your local café? ____________

p. 81/A2

3 ▶ The Golden Gate Bridge

Complete the crossword.

1 When the Forty-Niners left, Bodie became a … town.
2 The British say 'film', the Americans say '…'.
3 What's the fourth word?
hot - cold   warm - …
4 In 1848 the … Rush started in California.
5 Many black people weren't free – they were … .
6 Bodie was a gold-… town.
7 The designer of the Golden Gate Bridge came from … .
8 The ground is shaking – it's an … .
9 You mustn't drive faster than 40 miles an hour. There's a … .
10 What's the … today?
– It's 30°C.
11 You use a search engine to find something on the … .
12 A hot, dry area.
13 The place where they make films.
14 This is what you want most of all if you aren't free.
15 You write '25°C'. You say '25 … Celsius'.
16 What's the fourth word?
live - life   die - …

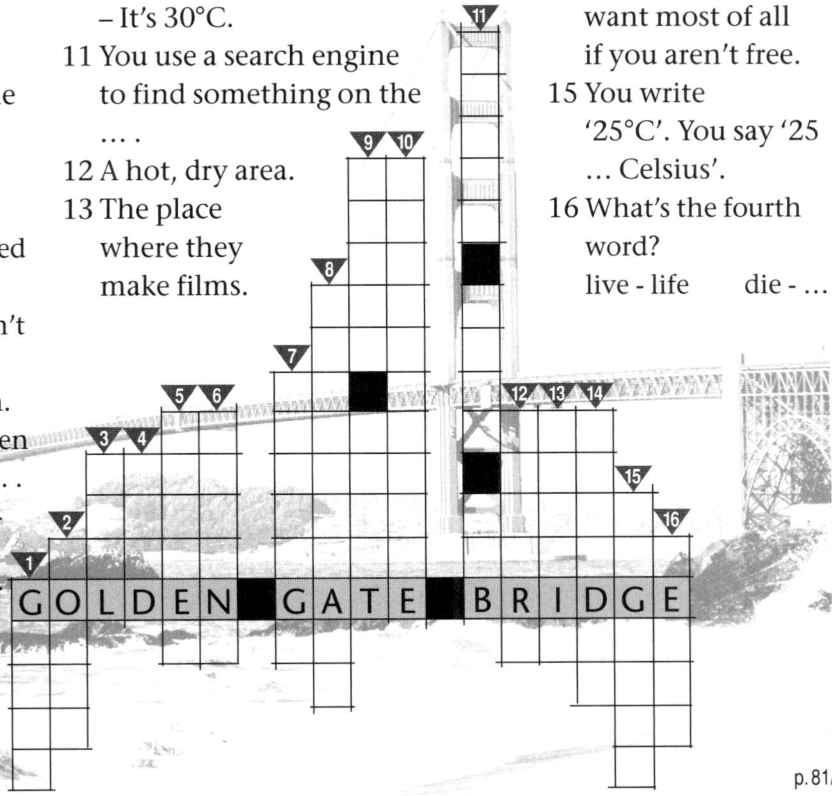

p. 81/A2

4 ▶ Questions, questions

You 'meet' an Italian boy in a chat room. His family has just moved to California. Write these questions to him.

1 When – move – America?

____

2 Why – leave Italy?

____

3 like California?

____

4 What Italian things – miss?

____

5 visit Italy sometimes?

____

6 Have – brothers and sisters?

____

7 speak English or Italian – home?

____

8 go – American school?

____

▶▶▶ NOW YOU

What else can you ask the Italian boy? Write five more questions in your exercise book.

p. 81/A2

5 ▶ Add words

Use the symbols ∗ and ◊ to show where you could put the words on the left in the sentences on the right. (Sometimes there is more than one possibility.)

1 probably ∗	She'll be here on Saturday afternoon .
2 at about 3 pm ∗	I'll meet her at the station .
3 usually ∗	The train is late .
4 ever ∗	I don't think my town will change .
5 always ∗	It will be the same .
6 a bit ∗ ; sometimes ◊	I get bored .
7 quite ∗; really ◊	But it's nice .
8 actually ∗; perfectly ◊	I'm happy here .

p. 82/A3

6 ▶ Explaining traditions

Complete this conversation at the Tet Festival in San Francisco.

GERMAN TOURIST Hast du eine Ahnung, worum es hier geht? Warum werden diese ganzen Knallkörper angezündet? Du sprichst doch Englisch. Frag doch mal den Mann da.

YOU Excuse me, ____?

VIETNAMESE AMERICAN We always light them at Tet. They are against evil spirits.

YOU ____

GERMAN TOURIST Frag ihn, was für ein Fest sie gerade feiern.

YOU ____

VIETNAMESE AMERICAN It's the Vietnamese spring festival. It's called Tet.

YOU ____

____

VIETNAMESE AMERICAN You're from Germany, aren't you? What traditions do you have?

YOU Er will wissen, ____.

GERMAN TOURIST Eine gute Frage …

▶▶▶ NOW YOU

Think of a tradition that people in your area have. How would you explain it to a foreigner?

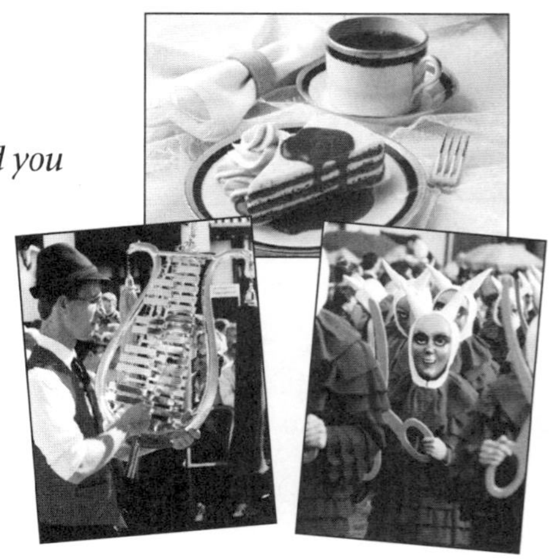

____

____

____

____

____

p. 83/A5

WORKING WITH THE TEXT

7 ▶ What does it really mean?

Find these sentences in the text on pages 88–90 of your pupil's book.
What exactly do they mean? Choose from the ideas below.

1 Well, she's not exactly my girlfriend.	a Rodney would like Ivy to be his girlfriend.	☑
	b Rodney doesn't want Ivy to be his girlfriend.	☐
2 Guys like Lavell Tyler don't breathe the same air as guys like me.	a Rodney thinks he's better than Lavell.	☐
	b Rodney thinks Lavell is better than him.	☐
3 When Ivy came into class, she looked like someone had died.	a Ivy looked very upset.	☐
	b Ivy told Rodney someone has died.	☐
4 'I felt like a total idiot!'	a Ivy felt a bit silly when she saw Lavell and Deleisha.	☐
	b Ivy felt very silly when she saw Lavell and Deleisha.	☐
5 'I told him what he could do with that idea!'	a Ivy said it was no problem if Lavell sees Deleisha too.	☐
	b Ivy told Lavell she didn't want to see him any more.	☐
6 Music, that was what those words were.	a Rodney hears music.	☐
	b Rodney is very happy.	☐
7 'You stay reliable, you hear what I'm saying, Rodney?'	a Ivy wanted a boyfriend who doesn't go out with other girls.	☐
	b Ivy wanted a boyfriend who is cool.	☐

8 ▶ Guess what happened yesterday!

Rodney often writes e-mails to his friends. Read through the text again and imagine what he wrote on the days these things happened.

My girlfriend (?!)

From...
To... Raymond
Subject: My girlfriend (?!)

I know this girl called Ivy. I went with her to the pizza place today.

____

____

ATT Night!

From...
To... Benny; Bobby W.
Subject: ATT Night!

Hey guys, I can't believe what happened at the show yesterday!

____

____

____

____

pp. 88–90

9 ▶ ... talk about your dreams in English

How do you say these things in English?

1 Ich bin verrückt nach alten Kinofilmen.

____

2 Ich träume manchmal davon, Schauspieler/in zu werden.

____

____

3 Ich will viel Geld machen, wenn ich älter bin.

____

4 Ich frage mich, ob ich es schaffen werde.

____

5 Wird mein Traum wahr werden?

____

10 ▶ ... find the odd one out

One word in each group is different. (Circle) it. Can you add any words to the groups?

guitar	record	desert	actor
piano	classical	coast	singer
reggae	pop	valley	director
synthesizer	folk	bridge	special effects
violin	rock	mountain	camera person
________	________	________	________

11 ▶ ... write for the school newspaper

Have you seen a great film that you could tell other people about? Or heard a great song? Maybe you've seen a play or a concert? Or perhaps there's a great programme on TV that you think other people should watch? Write a short article like Julie's for the school newspaper.

Last week I went to a talent show. Lots of kids from our school were in it. Everybody was really good, but the best act was Ice Happa (Rodney Suyama and Ivy Ramos). Rodney did a rap and Ivy walked up and down with a drum. The best bit was when they both landed on the floor. It was the funniest thing I have ever seen! You can see them at our school talent show this week. Don't miss it!

Julie Muramoto

____

____

____

____

____

____

____

Unit 6 How to organize information for a presentation

1 ▶ Starting

a *First, look at the three texts on this page. You have to collect information about L.A.'s* ***climate***[1] *and* ***history*** *for a presentation. The useful information is underlined.*

[1] climate [ˈklaɪmət] *Klima*

From a travel guide

history

Until 1848 California was part of Mexico, when it was sold to the USA. That is why there is so much Spanish spoken there today. In 1848 and 1849 gold was discovered there. Thousands of people went west to California to try to find some. Today it is still called the 'golden state'. In 1850 California became the 31st American state.

The tourist industry is very important here. The area in and around L.A. offers a lot to people who have free time on their hands. Beach-lovers are at home there – they can go swimming, surfing, sailing and windsurfing. Fishing and rock climbing are also popular.

Believe it or not, you can also go skiing near L.A., from December until April.

But if you prefer to watch other people do the work, then go to one of the big baseball games (from April to October) or watch the L.A. Lakers, the famous basketball team.

From a web site

Favoriten | Verlauf | Suchen

You can go to L.A. at any time during the year – winter or summer. August and September are the hottest months when temperatures can reach 32 °C. January and February are the coolest and wettest months. But winter temperatures are not cold – they are often around 12 °C. The average temperature is 21 °C. If you go to L.A. in the summer, the beaches will be very full. If you want to visit one of the national parks, you should book. They are busy too.

climate

From a multimedia encyclopedia

climate

Los Angeles is famous for its nice weather, films and TV industry, earthquakes, fires and smog.

history

It was founded in 1781 by a group of Spaniards. The railway arrived in the 1870s and the city began to grow. By 1900 the population had reached 100,000. In 2000 it was 3.5 million.

Today L.A. is one of the most important centres of industry in the USA. Electronic equipment, clothes, food and chemicals are produced there. The city is also famous for its space industry.

b *Use these headings. Make notes for the talk in your exercise book.*

climate:	history
hottest time: ...	1781: ...
temp.: ...	1848/49: ...
coolest time: ...	1850: ...
temp.: ...	1870s: ...
ave. temp.: ...	1900: ...
nice	2000: ...

2 ▶ The next step

Your next job is to make notes about ***industry*** *and* ***outdoor activities*** *in L.A.*

a *Read through the three texts again. Underline the important points for these topics and write* ***industry*** *or* ***outdoor activities*** *next to them.*

b *Make notes about them.*

c *Use your notes. Practise giving a short talk (2–3 minutes only).*

Revision (Units 4–6)

1 ▶ Conditional sentences, type II

A class is discussing where they want to go on a trip. What are they saying?

At Frederick Sound in Alaska, you can often see 50 whales at one time.

Highest temperatures in Florida in the summer are about 32 degrees.

In Death Valley, nothing grows. The only animals are rabbits and wild sheep.

Yosemite National Park is full of wonderful animals – you can see bears and 60 other different animals. Also in Yosemite you can see giant trees, huge waterfalls, and the highest mountain in the US, after Mount Denali – Mount Whitney.

1 go to Alaska / see some whales
If we went to Alaska, we would see some whales.

2 visit Florida / temperatures / be too high for me
If we ______________________________
______________________________.

3 choose Death Valley / not see any interesting animals
____
____
____

4 decide to go to Yosemite / see bears and giant trees
____
____

5 go to California / not see any whales
____
____

6 have time / also like to climb Mount Whitney
____
____

2 ▶ Comparatives and superlatives

Complete the text with the right form of the words in brackets.

In California everything is (big) __________ and (good) __________ than anywhere else. They have (tall) __________ trees in the world and (big) __________ films. They think that they have (good) __________ software developers in the world and (famous) __________ film stars. But they also have (hot) __________ place on earth and some people think they have (bad) __________ earthquakes, too.

Revision (Units 4–6)

3 ▶ Verbs with 'up'

Complete the sentences. Use the correct form of one of the verbs in the box and up.

cut • go • grow • look pick • put • shut • wake	+ up

1 I've never ________ this tent *up* before. Can you help me?
2 We bought a tent three years ago. Prices have ____________ a lot since then.
3 Dave is asleep again. ________ him ____!
4 Do you know the number of the Park Office?
– No, but we can ________ it ____ .
5 Can you ____________ that wood? We want to make a fire.
6 I've dropped my knife. Can you ________ it ____?
7 The boys in the next tent are so noisy. When are they going to ____________?
8 The boys are like babies sometimes. They should ____________ .

We put the tents up by a river.

4 ▶ Questions

One of the group met a very friendly park ranger, Julie. What questions did Julie ask?

1 Where – come from?
____
I come from Britain.
2 Who – arrange trip? ______________________________
My teachers arranged it. I'm here with my class from school.
3 USA – before? ______________________________
No, this is my first time in the USA.
4 enjoy? ______________________________
Yes, I'm having a wonderful stay.
5 How long? ______________________________
We've been here since last Friday.
6 bears? ______________________________
No, we haven't seen any bears, but we saw some bear tracks yesterday.
7 ______________________________
We go walking or cycling everyday, and we've been swimming once.
8 ______________________________
In the lake near the waterfall. The water was freezing!

Julie, the park ranger

5 ▶ Conditional sentences, type III

Debbie has had a terrible week. Complete the text.

On Monday I failed my Social Studies quiz. If I (do) *had done* more work the night before, I (pass) ______________________ . If (not, go) ______________ to that party on Saturday night, I (not, feel) ______________________ so tired on Sunday. On Monday Dad forgot to pick me up from band practice. If I (call) ____________ him, he (not, forget) ______________________________ . On Tuesday I got home really late from Grandma's and Mom was mad. If I (tell) ___________ her where I was going, she (not, be) _______________________ so mad. I wanted to go to a film on Friday, but I didn't have any money. I'd left it in my jeans. Dad washed them and the money got wet. If I (take) ____________ the money out, it (not, get) ______________________ wet.

6 ▶ Gerunds

Use gerunds *to make one sentence out of two.*

1 I don't want to listen to this song any more. I'm fed up with it.

I'm fed up with ____ .

2 I go out alone at night. I'm not scared.

I'm not scared of ____ .

3 My dad gave me a mobile phone. I thanked him.

I thanked my dad for ____ .

4 I'm going on holiday soon. I'm looking forward to that.

____

5 My parents don't want to move to a different country. They can't imagine it.

____

____

6 I'd love to go to New York. I often dream of that.

____

7 ▶ All about me

Answer this e-mail in your exercise book. Do you like the things Kelly likes? Tell her about the things you like, and the things you hate. Do you think you could be friends?

All about me

From...

To...

Subject: All about me

My name's Kelly Bayford and I'm a student at Kennedy High School, Hollywood, USA. I'm 14 years old and I enjoy doing sport, e.g. baseball and swimming. I also like watching Star Trek, eating spicy food, getting up early and going for long walks with my dog. Going to school is OK. I hate visiting museums and going camping :-(
Do you like the same things? Write and tell me all about yourself!
Kelly